My Football

Story

My Football Story

By: Wesley Eggleston

Illustrated by: Bonnie Lou Coleman

Acknowledgments

I would like to acknowledge Mr. Michael Schooler, my creative writing teacher from my junior year of high school. He told me this story would be one of the greatest pieces of literature I would write. He suggested one day I would open it up, randomly read it, and be inspired to add more. He predicted correctly. Nine years later, this narrative is something I take tremendous pride in. I converted the original ten-page personal narrative assignment, first considered a hassle, into a masterwork. Mr. Schooler not only challenged me to be creative, he opened my eyes to how many writers compose in cliché. To this day, he remains one of my favorite teachers and I owe a lot of my writing abilities, understanding the need to constantly expand words in my vocabulary weekly, drive, compassion, and giving me the start to what I turned into my first published book.

Had I not participated in his elective writing class, and had he not challenged me in the way he did, I would not have developed the skills, and knowledge to put this narrative together.

Second I would like to thank my illustrator, Bonnie Lou Coleman for her amazing artwork. While going through the process of hiring an illustrator, I knew right away when I had initial communication with Ms. Bonnie that she was someone who shared my vision, and passion for making this book a reality. Her attention to detail, commitment, and drive to read and illustrate scenes only made my book better. For this I thank her and I am eternally grateful!

Lastly, but not least I would also like to thank my family for all their encouragement and support. They saw my gift long before I did, and kept pointing me in the right direction. It is through them, and God, that making this book a published reality was possible. Since my childhood they saw I had a knack for writing. My resulting grades and ability to successfully present papers, stories, and articles, etc. have proven that. I love every last member of my family who also helped make this book happen. I hope this story helps build awareness and understanding for those who read it.

Football Dictionary and further reading on

subject matter included.

My Football Story

I was done. After eight long years of basketball I felt it was time for a change. I was getting ready to start a new chapter in my life, high school. I thought, *'new grade level, why not try a new sport?'*

I had always lived in the shadow of people telling me, "Wesley you know if you ever decided to play football you would probably make out to be a good player."

You see, my dad and his old high school football buddies always hook up for the Super Bowl, or a New Year's Eve Party. They si and reminisce on the good ole' days. Teasing each other about how they would always try to knock each other around during their football practices. Dad was an all-purpose player who did everything! He played offense, defense and special teams his senior season. His two closest friends, the ones who teased me the most in my youth, are Mr. Andre and Mr. Lorenzo. When Mr. Lorenzo played, he was the agile, '*I'll beat you with my speed,*' running back. Mr. Andre was more of the bruising, potent running back that loved to beat up other players with his strength.

I never paid much attention to Dad's friends because football seemed like too much pain to me. I had a favorite NFL team, the St. Louis Rams, now Los Angeles. My all time favorite player is, now retired, running back, Steven Jackson. I say that loosely because I was only familiar with them from video games. I had rarely, if at all, watched them play an actual game. One could call me a fair weather fan, though I took

pride in claiming the Rams as my favorite football team. A reasonable

person would think the passion from playing football video game titles

like NFL Blitz, and the popular Madden franchise, for years would

translate to wanting to play the real game. I didn't like the thought of

hitting anyone in a repetitive manner.

Since I was in desperate need of change, I decided

to try it out. I finally gave into the notion of going out for the team when

a bunch of my close friends said that they would be trying out for their

prospective high school teams. Looking back at the time I made my

decision, Dad still jokes about how it came to be.

***

All of the new freshmen had our first practice and meeting with the coach on a fresh summer afternoon at Saint Elizabeth High School. I was definitely scared, yet eager for what lay ahead. I wanted to make a good first impression and establish myself as a promising player early. When I got out of the car I saw a guy patiently waiting by a railing. The railing appeared to lead under ground.

The guy was Coach Robinson, an African American

male, about six feet tall and in his forties. He was definitely in shape; after all, he was a football coach. He wore a hat to hide his nearly balding head and glasses to shade his grizzly bear brown eyes.

"Hello, are you Coach Robinson?" I asked, approaching him with a little bit of nervousness in my throat.

He replied in his deep, and welcoming voice, "Yes I am. What is your name?"

"My name is Wesley Eggleston. It is nice to meet you," I said with a huge smile. I finally asked the question that had been playing pinball in my mind during our brief encounter, "Are we going to be in gear today coach?"

"No we have to get you guys in shape before we even step foot on the field in pads."

I concluded we were probably about to do some running. Once everyone arrived for our first session Coach Robinson wanted us to warm up. I made sure my shoes were laced and prepared to take on two laps around what looked like a miniature version of a track. I was juiced, so I took off, like a robber who stole diamonds from a jewelry store.

After the two laps we went into an underground chamber- like room. It was like a basement designed for lifting weights. I was amazed by the size of it. I had never been in a real weight room before. All of the machines and specialized equipment were overwhelming. The walls were a dirty snow color, probably from previous players who rubbed up against them. Hanging on the walls were instructions on how to lift certain weights, in case someone forgot the routine. Anyone using the machines could easily look to the explanations and instructions. The smell of rubber, rusted metal and sweat instantly filled my nose when I entered the room. I was expecting brand new weight equipment. In truth, cavemen probably used the same weight sets we were using.

The thought of getting stronger had not even crossed my mind up to that point. I had only lifted weights once before with Dad. That was a mess because I was so weak. I didn't care to embarrass myself on the first day. What a way to start off high school sports. The question of why I signed up for football fluttered in the back of my mind. I wasn't regretting the fact that I signed up for football already, was I? I hadn't even officially gotten into it yet. I didn't want to judge the sweetness of the Kool-Aid before I tasted it.

Coach Robinson needed our measurements to keep in his records. He tracked our weight, how much we were lifting, and many other little things he wanted to keep a record of. I got my measurements in; weight 205 pounds, height 5'8.

After Coach Robinson acquired our measurements, he started us off on the bench press. We went in alphabetical order. When it was my turn my heart started beating like a chef who beats some breakfast eggs, really hard. I lied down and did exactly as he instructed the others who bench-pressed before me. Grip the bar by the crow's feet, and push up. The bar was only forty-five pounds, and even though I lifted more than forty-five pounds while taking in the groceries for my mom, I was impressed I could lift it. I did the number of reps that were required, and then watched the others finish up. We then moved to the next weight-training piece. After being able to lift the bench press, I was feeling good about myself.

"What's next coach?" I asked with confidence.

"The next thing we will try you guys out on is the incline."

It was similar to the bench press, yet the upper half of the bench was raised to create an incline. The rest of my teammates completed their reps; when it was my turn, I was ready. The same techniques applied, except one is supposed to lift the bar over their eyes and back down to their chest to complete a full rep. I lifted the bar over my eyes, and then to my surprise, when I was coming down to my chest, the bar fell down on my lap.

"Dang, get this bar off me!"

It was like I had the weight of a bowling ball resting on my lap, (any man could relate.) Coach Robinson and a few others rushed to get the bar off of my lap. He explained to me what I did wrong and how to avoid a repeat of the incident in the future. I realized that I put the bar too far over the position it should be in when in the air coming down, which is why it fell onto my lap. Of course, every time I did the incline from that point on I feared dropping the bar on my lap again. Every now and then I did drop the bar and with time I had the strength to pull it up before disaster struck.

***

After a month and a half, I learned to love weight training. It was a great experience for me. I found strength inside myself that I never knew I had. I could go around talking like I was a hard-core body builder. The weight piece I had truly fallen in love with was the squat-lift. This is, honestly, the contraption in which you put the weight of the world on your shoulders. You put the weights on the bar, you put the bar on your back, and then you do a repetition of squats. I loved this weight lifting exercise because I was good at it. I always believed I had a sturdy upper back. As long as I took the proper precautions, I could do no wrong.

***

It was a hot afternoon when Coach Robinson said we were going to max out on the squat lift. I observed a sophomore named Lawrence Nishmura doing his squats and witnessed the technique and form he used. He got as low as he could, and then thrust upwards as fast as possible. Lawrence's

technique was very smooth and seemingly simple, even though it is a

difficult skill to learn. I looked up to Lawrence because he was the kind

of person who knew how to take criticism and do what the coach asked,

even if it was harsh. That was how I wanted to be. I thought if coach

was putting that kind of reliance on Lawrence in his second year,

maybe in my second year I could fulfill some of the same

responsibilities. Coach Robinson wanted Lawrence to be a leader on

and off the field, for games and in practices. As an adolescent player, I

looked to him for guidance.

Lawrence Nishmura was Asian American,

heavy-set in his body makeup, and solid. He was

very well spoken and always encouraging. He was clean cut most of the time, with a smile on his face.

When it was my turn to max out, I repeatedly said to myself: '*Come on Wes, you can do this*!' I completed the first rep, moved on to the second and then the third. Everyone in the room started taking notice of me. They were all watching and cheering me on, which boosted my confidence and gave me an added adrenaline rush. I maxed out at two hundred and twenty-five pounds.

'*How the heck am I going to squat this with everyone watching me? I'm gonna mess up if I don't do this right,*' I thought to myself.

"Wesley, at the amount of weight you are squatting, it is important that your technique is

right, or you will hurt your back," Coach Robinson said, with what
sounded like a hint of concern.

Good form!

Way to go!

Great job Wesley!

Keep it up!

You got it man!

Everyone had picked up the cheering again by chanting my
name repeatedly as I was attempting to hit the weight. I went to squat
the bar, but my back gave out before I could fully pull off the rep.
Coach gave me a second try, and nothing changed from my first result.
Coach seemed to be

pleased I had moved that far up in weight, so I never thought twice about not being able to that day. The fact that everyone watched and supported me while I attempted to lift the weights was the first time I felt I was slowly gaining respect from the whole Mustang football family.

I started to get a feel for what professional athletes preseason training felt like. I was sorer than an old man in a retirement home. I could barely hold a brush to fix my hair in the morning, or lift my fork at the dinner table. I had worked so hard. All the same, I was honestly excited for more; like a kid ready for another thrilling ride at Disneyland.

***

With school starting in a few weeks, and summer workouts winding down, I couldn't wait for the season to start. It was either going to make a man out of me or I was going to collapse

down like Goliath.

Apparently the Friday before this particular Monday practice, Coach Robinson made an announcement he was taking his varsity players to a special skills camp. They would be attending with other varsity teams in the Bay Area for the entire week. Most important, the JV team had the week off. I didn't get the memo.

I was rushing up to St. Liz bracing myself for another day on the gridiron when I noticed everything was in place except for one thing, no JV players at all! There were only varsity players waiting around for Coach Robinson to get there. When Coach Robinson pulled up in his car I walked over to him.

Before I could say anything he asked, "Wesley what are you doing here?"

"I'm here for practice. Doesn't JV practice today?" I asked with confusion.

"No, I gave you guys the week off because the varsity team is going to a skills camp. We were actually supposed to be there right now, but they cancelled today. We will be going the rest of the week. So no practice for you all."

"Oh okay," I said feeling kind of stupid for not paying attention.

Before I could say '*Bye, see you next week*,' Coach Robinson said, "Wes, since you're already here, and we will be on our regular practice field working today, you might as well stay and get some extra work in."

He phrased it as an option, and I knew by declining his invitation it would be interpreted as a sign of laziness. I did not want Coach Robinson to think of me like that. I was so underdeveloped with my knowledge of the game and fundamentals that this day of practice was probably a gift from God.

Coach told me all his staff would be attending the camp. That day I got to meet the varsity offensive line coach, Coach Davis. Coach Davis had a heavy midsection and was less than six feet in height. Coach Davis sported a thick toothbrush bristle mustache filled with a sporadic amount of gray and fading black hairs. This was my opportunity to show him what I could do at the next level. Not only him, but all the coaches, and even some of the older veteran players.

The coaches told the varsity players to line up with a different coach based on their position. Coach Davis and Coach Montenes took all the linemen to work with them.

Coach Montenes was a Mexican American man in his late-twenties with a couple of tattoos across his arm. He had a grin on his face that let you know he meant business. He was cool to talk to, as I soon found out.

Coach Davis and Coach Montenes took all the linemen over to an area of the field where there was enough room to do drills and run. We weren't in any gear, so I was clueless about what to expect. I was under the impression I was there to observe the varsity players doing their routines more than I was going to be participating anyway. I wasn't expecting to stand out like I was a top player.

The first drill Coach Montenes and Coach Davis had us do was similar to what I had done in basketball for years. It was a form of a three-man weave. In football though, there was no running around the person a player passed the ball to, and keep cutting to the middle to make a weave down a court. This version of the three-man weave for football required three players to lie on their stomachs and jump and roll over the next player and keep moving until the coaches said stop. The person in the middle would be up off the ground slightly.

When the coaches said go, the middle person would

jump over the player rolling to the right. Then the third person would be rolling to get ready to move to the spot for the jump and keep the drill going in a rapid circuit. I was watching this with my own eyes. I could see the resemblance to the basketball version of the three-man weave, yet I was still confused. Coach Davis and Coach Montenes let the varsity players go through the exercise a couple of times. I know they noticed me avoiding the drill by standing in the back of all the varsity players.

Finally Coach Davis yelled without locating where I was standing, "Alright Wesley, get up here, and let's see something!"

I stepped tensely through the crowd of varsity players like Simba's slow walk after Mufasa scolded him for disobeying his orders in The Lion

King. I started on the end where I was to roll first. That part I knew. When it came to jumping up and moving out of the way, clearing the player rolling underneath me, my body was still, like a frozen computer screen. This of course caused the varsity players doing the drill with me to look at me funny as if questioning why I didn't keep up. They didn't say anything, but their smirks said it all.

> Then Coach Davis expressed it to me verbally "This is an agility drill son, get up and move out the way when you clear!"

I didn't have a response. I knew I didn't do my part in the drill right. My body was at a standstill for some reason when it was time to jump over, and then roll again. Three times in a row he let me go, and all three times my body didn't want to move. In my mind I knew I wasn't going to hear the end of it from my coaches.

Coach Davis pulled me up and shouted in my face this time, "This is an agility exercise son. You're going to have to move your body. Quit messing up my drill!"

When he got in my face, I was afraid. My eyes widened as if I saw a baseball coming straight for me at a hundred miles an hour. He pushed me to the side to be in my thoughts. In a few minutes he told me to get back in the front of the line to try it again. I knew this time there was no choice. That fear of not wanting to do the drill was going to have to disappear quickly, like a mouse in its hole in the wall after being spotted. This time I was able to do it. I told myself that any punishment would be far worse than the drill itself. My group did the drill a few extra minutes. I knew it was because Coach Davis saw I was doing it correctly.

Coach Davis could see my work ethic in all the other drills during that practice too. When it was all said and done, I felt good about how much better I was from that day.

When I had a side conversation with Coach Davis, he expressed, "I wish you were older, and were able to go to this camp too. I could get some more work in with you. Coach Robinson doesn't feel you're ready for it though. Plus you're not old enough either, as I mentioned."

"It's okay," I said; lost for words. Were his comments based off the fact that I needed a lot of work, or did he really say it from the bottom of the soles of his shoes?

Based on this session alone, giving me confidence unknowingly, as we were all heading to the locker room when practice was over, I overheard Coach Davis tell Lawrence, "Look out for Wesley, he's going to be a special player."

Those comments made me feel good inside.

I knew that with those comments though, I would have to keep my intensity level up. I wanted to live up to Coach Davis's claim. It wasn't like he knew I had heard what he said, still knowing that I did hear him, made me not want to let him down. More importantly I did not want to let myself down.

***

The day before high school started, Coach Robinson and the other coaches told us all to wait in the locker room after practice before we went home. It was finally time for him to give us our pads and equipment. I had become so strong in my arms, legs, and mind, I envisioned myself going up against some of the greats in NFL history like Jackie Ray Slater, who was one of the best offensive linemen to play in football. While playing his entire career with the St. Louis Rams, he totaled over two hundred games and put up some nice stats too. If I could establish myself as a good player, I knew I could fit in on the field. I had put in all the work thus far, and I wasn't going to settle for the last slice of pepperoni pizza. With all that I endured; taking the BART in the afternoon, racing to practice so I wouldn't be late, and blowing off plans to go to the movies with my friends, all to show up for practice, I was going to make sure I got playing time in the games.

Football equipment and gear consisted of; a helmet to protect your head, a mouthpiece to protect your mouth, teeth, and tongue, thigh pads, hip pads, and gloves. Another item made necessary by Coach Davis was a jockstrap although it wasn't required to play. I had everything I needed to get out on the field.

***

The most important responsibility of an offensive lineman is to protect the most important position in the sport, the quarterback. Our JV quarterbacks' name was Juan Bell. He was one of the most popular kids in our freshmen class, let alone on the JV squad. Off the field he wore glasses, and typically had his hair in various style: curly, straightened, or braided. He was African American and Mexican mix. He respected me on and off the field as a teammate and as an acquaintance however, we were never super close. We had a couple of classes together during the school year. We even sat next to each other in our freshman math class, but we would never go out of our way to hang out with each other outside of football. Having the quarterback's trust went a long way in the sense that if we, as linemen, didn't do our jobs in keeping him upright, he wouldn't be able to do his job to deliver the ball to open receivers down the field.

Hitting in pads was painful. To me, the worst part about practice was the fact that during our drills we had to go up against the juniors and seniors with a few sophomores who made the varsity team like Lawrence, for stents. These were some big boys on the varsity offensive and defensive line. The biggest of them all was Charles Davis, or as he like to be called by his peers "C.D."

C.D. was African American. He was huge and made us JV linemen look like dimes compared to a half dollar. He had a wide frame, built like a mammoth, with a roundish head that sat on his shoulders. He was at least three hundred pounds based strictly on one's eye. For the first couple of weeks I knew C.D., I thought he was a senior. It was not until midway through the season did I find out he was only a junior. During weight training he lifted the most out of everyone, and it wasn't by a couple of pounds either. He was ahead of the seniors by fifty or so pounds on some of the weight machines, (which furthered my speculation he had to be a senior). Sometimes when we were scrimmaging against the varsity players, (O) line against (D) line, my JV teammates and I would look across the other side of the line and blow over seeing C.D. huffing and puffing in front of us. I guess the coaches could care less about a raw freshmen going up against a huge junior or senior. Being new to football, and having to go up against experienced hard-hitting players frustrated me. The worst thing was that sometimes I'd get mild headaches along with the pain of a tackle.

Another player on varsity was a junior defensive lineman named Jerry Ali. Jerry had a country type accent when he spoke. Sometimes it was hard to take him seriously. He didn't play around when it came to football though, so laughing at him was not a smart choice. He only played defensive line, and was so high motor playing every down like it was his last. I knew it was one of the reasons he had to be on the field a lot. He made things happen on the field. During one of the head on, one on one, collision drills for linemen I had to go up against Jerry. I'll never forget it!

One of the varsity coaches, Coach Jones, was hyping Jerry up to really go at me, and not hold back. Coach Jones was the oldest of all the coaches, and the most 'old school' of them all. Meaning he had been around the sun more than any other coach, and seen more in life than anyone else. He still had plenty of energy for an assistant football coach. He knew what he was teaching, so players respected him. Even though sometimes his old school references during practices would leave players confused. We tried to keep our heads down and made sure he never caught us slipping. He would call players on every mistake, in a fashion that only an older football coach could.

Coach Jones was tall, had a tooth or two missing, and a graying mustache. He was bald and wore a hat all the time to hide it.

"Blow his ass up Jerry!" Coach Jones demanded.

What else could I do, but brace myself and try to maintain my position? I knew what was coming my way from an aggressive guy like Jerry. The best thing to do was just keep grinding away, getting back up if I got knocked down, and maintain my position even if it was going to be the death of me.

***

Coach Davis desire for me to follow Lawrence's lead provided me an interesting situation. He was subtly making sure of it. Coach Davis needed Lawrence to move from his guard position to play center. Simultaneously he wanted me to try out for the position of center on the JV team. Center is a part of the offensive line responsible for giving the ball to the quarterback before maintaining their blocking assignment.

Coach Davis told me to practice the motion of playing center at home too. He told me to practice by taking a toilet paper roll and snapping it under my legs. Coach Davis would pull Juan and I away from team practice sometimes, so we could practice our snaps together.

"We gotta pick up our speed," said Juan.

I took this opportunity seriously because next to playing quarterback, center was a key position. I always found time before bed to take a roll of toilet paper and get a few repetitions in before I slept. I wanted it to be my new permanent position instead of moving back to guard.

Unfortunately my timing was never consistently

quick enough. My short tryout for center was over within two weeks. I was glad for the opportunity to test out and see if it fit me. It meant my skills were being evaluated by all my coaches, as opposed to not getting considered at all for a role.

***

A lot of stamina is required when playing football. It is one thing to be in shape as an athlete. Saying a person is in football shape is a whole different flavor of ice cream. The training, preparation, and self-motivation a player has to embrace to go through the motions are challenging. I became more cognizant of these challenges with every practice. I would do what I called, '*psyche myself in,*' a routine I had practiced my whole life in a variety of situations. I would give myself a million reasons why I couldn't do something. Then when the moment came I would react naturally and do it!

Even when the task was something as simple sounding as getting the water in the coolers and carrying them to our practice field (a chore all freshen had to endure), was something that needed mental preparation. Cleaning out the coolers, carrying them to the side of the school to fill with water, then carrying them out to the practice field. All that, and we still had to be on time for practice when the coaches were ready to start. The water wasn't good drop for drop, but sometimes after long practice session with tackling in the hot sun, water never tasted so good!

***

Football is a violent game. A person must know this before ever stepping on a field. This was certainly one of the reasons I avoided the sport for years. The demands of football can cause people to lose their head. Fights can occur on and off the field from practices, to actual games. Some fights even take place in the locker room while players are changing in or out of their street clothes. It is part of the football culture. Sometimes teammates, or opposing players on separate teams, can lose their grips on life. When teammates fight it is usually over something silly. Many times a player loses their head and gets caught up in the situation. No one wants to look like a punk in front of an entire football team.

***

St. Elizabeth High School is a small school. So much so that it does not have a huge football field on site like most high school campuses in the Bay Area has, like a Bishop O'Dowd in Oakland, or St. Ignatius College Preparatory high school, in San Francisco.

St. Elizabeth only has a small grass field in the back of the school. Soccer players had to use it, PE classes used it, and certainly the football teams had to use it. The field was good enough for small games; still it was not big enough to call a regulation size field for any sport. In terms of preparing for actual football, there came a time when practicing on that field wasn't going to cut it.

There is a field about two miles away from Saint Elizabeth known as Curt Flood field. It is named after the famous baseball player, Curt Flood, who is best known for his unsuccessful suit against Major League Baseball's reserve clause. This is the clause, which binds a player to his team, even after his contract runs out.

The JV team had the luxury of riding in vans up to the field, while the varsity team had to sweat out a run there. When we first started riding in the vans, I for one was relieved. Warming-up on the small field, then having to gather up my stuff to run to Curt Flood, practicing, then run back following practice was daunting. One would like for things to stay the same, yet there is always something destined to change.

***

It was a regular day of studying in classes and dealing with the daily routines of school. As players were filing into the locker room to start changing for practice, two of my JV teammates were arguing. It was loud enough for everyone to hear. The arguing eventually led to a punch being thrown, leading to an all out fight between the two. While these two were fighting some players were either watching and egging them on, or like me, kept minding their own business and continuing to get ready for practice. This altercation lasted a few minutes before word eventually reached the coaches that players were fighting. The coaches rushed down and stopped the fight immediately.

Coach Robinson was furious that a fight broke out. Deep in my gut, I could feel what was coming next. Coach Robinson was about to unleash, and transform into what we called '*Raged*

Robinson!' He told everyone to hurry up and clear the locker room.

"Why were you two fighting?" Coach Robinson started off, along with a few other choice words that would not be aired over FCC airwaves.

He then directed a question to the whole football program, "If they were fighting how come no one went to hold them back from hitting each other?"

It got real quiet as eyes widened and heads bowed. No one really had a clear-cut answer to his questions. He went on to say a few other choice words. The other coaches also scolded us for being spectators. And boom, another hardship was laid out in front of us. When the reason came out for their fight, it couldn't have been more stupid. Their whole episode was over an ear pad that one of them thought the other player had stolen from their helmet.

I can't remember Coach Robinson's whole speech, or repeat most of it, nevertheless when he concluded, he said, "...I can't believe this whole fight was over something as stupid as an ear pad! So y'all all gonna pay for this! Everyone, including JV, take off running to the field!"

It was in that moment a new dynamic came about for the JV team. Instead of cruising in the vans up to Curt Flood, while the varsity team hustled to practice, we had to chug along up to the field with them. The whole St. Elizabeth football program was running to and from Curt Flood field from that point on, and it was something everyone on JV had to come to terms with.

When we passed everyday pedestrians, sometimes they would shout to us, "Man, your coaches have y'all training like y'all in the Marines!"

To ensure that everyone wasn't messing around taking their time walking, or going slow to get to the field, coaches would hide on different street corners to observe who was walking, and who was running. If we stopped running to walk for even a second because we thought we were in the clear from the coaches, without fail they would pop up like a jack-in-the-box and yell out the window, "That's fifty up-downs when you get to the field!"

Maybe there would have been a point later in the season when the JV coaches would have liked us to run to the field. For the long run to start happening over a fight about a missing ear pad was ridiculous!

I even reflected back to what Coach Herman Boone said in the movie *Remember The Titans*, when he addressed his football team after a fight between teammates. "You look like a bunch of fifth grade sissies after a cat fight! You got anger? That's good. You're gonna need it son. You got aggression? That's even better. You're gonna need that too. But any little two-year old child can throw a fit! Football is about controlling that anger, harnessing that aggression into a team effort to achieve perfection!"

That message held true for the Titan football team, and if it had been said to our team the words would have rang true for us too. We all spent so much time tackling and being aggressive in between the lines of the field that wasting our time fighting off the field was counterproductive.

***

In my opinion the hardest tackler on varsity was a guy named Dewayne Thompson. Dewayne was African American, slender, and as physical a running back as they came. He delivered pain like a mailman delivered the mail. He wasn't roadrunner fast, but he always managed to get extra yards using his power. He was the Captain of the varsity team, which meant he also had authority over the JV team too. Dewayne did his job, keeping people in line, and always performing above standards. I can honestly say I did not like him because he didn't give me the respect I felt I deserved. I knew I was only a freshman. Regardless I felt he should have shown my JV teammates and I a little more respect with the way he spoke to us.

One time, while I was getting my cleats laced up and was putting on an ankle brace after completing my run to Curt Flood; my ankle brace got caught in a knot. I had to sit down and redo the laces on the brace and then put it on, following my cleats. With no interruptions this could have easily took me all of two minutes to do.

Dewayne saw me sitting down, not even realizing what I was trying to do and yelled, "Get up, and don't sit back down!"

"I will as soon as I fix my shoes," I told him, rolling my

eyes.

He yelled again as he started to walk away, "Get up man!"

I shoved him and said, "I'll get up when I'm done fixin' this

bruh!"

Now I had done it! Maybe it was the hot sun above, or the

mere fact that it was probably going to be a long practice anyway, but

after I shoved Dewayne, he, of course, came back and shoved me.

Before long, I was in my own football fight. It didn't last long since

players pulled us apart, fortunately. I wasn't trying to fight Dewayne

anyway, as strong as he was. I did need to show him I wasn't going to

back down though. Luckily the coaches were off to the side having a

discussion

about what we were going to do during practice. They didn't notice.

Dewayne and I left it alone for the rest of that practice. I didn't forget that practice though. I believed that Dewayne had, even if a little, a thing against me. I kept my guard up around him after that. The way I was raised, as long as one person respects another, they should expect the same in return.

***

I got used to practicing against the varsity team after a while. Really it was my only option. If Coach Robinson ever suspected that we were going soft, he'd have some form of "punishment" waiting for us, whether it was running or doing up-downs. Up-downs are the worst simple drill football coaches ever created! We were only forced to do up- downs if we got in trouble with something related to school, or they were incorporated into one of the drills. It could be a drill where we had to hit the football sled, do an up down, roll over and hit the next dummy on the sled. Regardless of how they were designed, up-downs were a part of the practice all the time. I tried my best not to get poor grades, though they came and went and I had to take my punishment.

***

Our first game was in a week. We had to make sure we knew most of our plays so we could run them efficiently during the game. It was confusing to me how each hole in the offensive line had to open up. I knew it wasn't a critical match of chess, yet I still found it challenging when I was tired and couldn't think straight. Once again I was an offensive lineman; or a "fat boy", as Coach Montenes sometimes referred to us.

I played right guard, the position one spot over from the center. My teammate, Antwoine Campbell, played right tackle, the spot next to me. Antwoine was the strongest on the JV line and he was real smart too. Before every play started, I would always covertly ask him the type of play it was. He would oblige, whether it was a blocking play, a play where we had to open up a hole for the running back, or a play where we had to knock the defensive lineman straight on his butt. This made it seem like I knew what I was doing, even though sometimes I didn't. I was good at what I did, so me asking Antwoine prior to the start of the play didn't hurt the team in any way. Problems with my method only occurred if I didn't get word of what to do before the play started. I was left relying on my own instincts. I took chances that hopefully didn't lead to any type of penalty. Eventually though, I knew I would have to understand my job for plays without asking for help.

There are different stances and techniques for linemen that I had to get used to. Offensive linemen have to be in a three-point stance. When I first heard the term, I thought that it meant three fingers. So for a while, that's what I put down on the ground. The techniques varied depending on what side of the line someone was on. If a player played on the left side of the line, their techniques would work in mirror to those playing on the right.

Another skill linemen had to learn was the four-point stance. The

four-point stance was for defensive linemen.

Playing on the line, or in the trenches as it is referred to sometimes, has its

typical pros and cons. For example; an offensive lineman can't hold on to

his opponent, whereas a defensive linemen is able

to grab onto the oppositions jersey in pursuit of sacking the other team's quarterback.

* * *

The final Friday practice before Saturday's game came to an end. On Friday's we were never in full pads, only in our helmet, shorts, and tennis shoes. Although we had all gone over the offense and the defense, coach never announced who would be starting. He was going to tell us the starters for the game at the end of practice. The coaches announced from the jump that whoever worked the hardest would get a spot. We were all excited about what the next day would bring.

Now let me clarify Coach Robinson wasn't my official coach. There were seven coaches total, all part of the varsity staff during varsity games. However, during JV games two of the coaches stood in as head coach, and assistant coach:

Coach Montenes and Coach B.J. Coach Montenes were not as seasoned as Coach Robinson, but he could keep the intensity level up. He was a former student player for coach Robinson when he attended St. Liz. Coach B.J., a real funny guy, also didn't play around. He was a short man, shorter than me. He had a welcoming personality that made me feel comfortable going over things learned on the field with him. He was my favorite coach because he always acknowledged how hard I worked in practice. He also kept me sane whenever I got too down on myself.

When it was finally time at the end of practice for Coach Montenes to announce who would be starting on offense, my heart was still like a parked car. He announced who the running backs, the quarterback, wide receivers, and all the other positions were before he finally came to the offensive linemen. Of course, Antwoine's name was called first. Coach went through a couple of other names, and then finally said my name!

I yelled like a banshee, "Let's go!"

I had done it! I earned my spot on the starting offensive line.

Next came the starting defensive line. Coach Montenes named the players, though by this time it was obvious who was on that unit. Unfortunately, one of the players who was supposed to be on the starting defensive line wasn't at practice that day. He was one of the team's best defensive linemen on JV. Coach Montenes had a decision to make about who would get his spot for the time being. I assertively volunteered with the anticipation that I was going to be on the offensive and defensive line for the game. I had been practicing both. I knew the position, however, I felt more comfortable playing on the offensive line. Little did I know what I had set in motion.

***

Friday night I could barely sleep. Dad tried calming me down a couple of times. My heart slowly picked up momentum like a BART train taking off to the next station. I went to bed with a smile on my face and feathers tickling my insides. When I awoke the next morning, I showered and dressed for the game. I took care of everything that I had to do in my daily morning routine. My parents loaded everything in the car and drove me to school, where all of my teammates would be waiting for me.

When we got there I jumped out of the car and went straight down to the locker room to get all my equipment out of my locker. My parents were going to drive to the game separately.

"Hey, Coach Robinson and Coach Montenes how are you this morning? Are you guys ready for the games?"

"We are, how about you, Wes?"

"Yeah, I am. It took me a while to fall asleep last night, still I know I am ready for this!"

"Well get your pads and stuff and meet me upstairs so we can go over last minute things before we head to the bus," Coach Montenes said.

I got my pads and headed straight upstairs. We got in line as Coach Montenes yelled out what formation he wanted in front of him for a walk through.

"Starting offensive get out here!"

I was thinking, '*yeah, that's all me!*'

Since I didn't do the full review session on offense the previous day,

Coach Montenes didn't want me in the starting offense. I was going

to say something, but I decided not to. I didn't want to be a

distraction. The focus needed to be on getting a win in a couple of

hours. Coach Montenes

obviously wanted me in the starting defense for the day. However, that wasn't his exact plan.

He called out the starting defense. The defensive lineman, the one I volunteered to cover for, was back now. Coach Montenes wanted him to have his spot back. I knew that player was a better defensive lineman than me; still I didn't think that was fair.

I guess, "fair is a place they judge pigs," as ESPN analyst Stephen A. Smith would say.

People who know me would say I am a happy person, with a smiling face all the time. When Coach Montenes arranged the starting lines for the field without including me I was pissed.

After our short dress rehearsal, we boarded the bus and were off to the game. On the ride over, I was as uiet as a garden gnome. People were excited and bragging about how they were going to perform in the game.

'*They did me so dirty,*' I thought to myself. '*I did all that mess, I ran those aching laps, and I should be on the field when the game starts.*'

My level of excitement had gone from the top of the Appalachian Mountains to the bottom of Australia. We got to the field and everyone started to warm-up. We had to win our first game. We had worked too hard to lose now. The game was about to kickoff and everyone who should have been on the field was there, except me.

The game started and we looked pretty decent. I was so heated that I didn't want anything to do with the game. I stood off to the side with a grimace on my face, underneath my helmet. I can definitely remember when my parents got to the game. As they passed me on their way to the bleachers they gave me an odd look.

"What's wrong?" Mom and Dad asked in unison?

"Nothing!" I said with a tone in my voice that would probably get me in trouble at home.

My parents didn't say anything else to me, yet, as always, they knew something was wrong. They had a spider sense for knowing when something was wrong with me. The first quarter went by with the score remaining at zero. Luckily the guy who had my starting offensive spot was messing up every now and then, and Coach Montenes was really starting to get on him. Late in the second quarter Coach Montenes finally called my name.

I hesitated for about five seconds thinking, 'W*hy should coach use me now*?' I swallowed my frustrations in an instant, and got out there to handle my business.

To say I went into the game and completely dominated right away would be a lie. As a matter of fact, the first two plays I was in there, the referees called out my number, *seventy*, for holding. I didn't know what holding was because of the aggressiveness I played with in practice, and the absence of a referee. With my lack of understanding of football rules, no one ever told me it wasn't allowed. After Coach Montenes yelled at me not to hold I had to adjust my blocking technique. To my credit, I was able to make those fixes quickly. It was an easy transition from that point on. I made my mark after that. I got to play the rest of the game. I made some nice blocks too. I was showing the coaches, with my actions, why I should have been in the game from the start. Even though we lost the game, I walked away having a ton of hubris.

***

Our first game hadn't gone the way we planned, we needed to work out our kinks to be successful moving forward. During every practice all of the coaches would tell us to come prepared to get better than we were the day before. I did this, and I was going to try to show all the coaches, even though I wasn't the best athlete, I was lways ready to put in work. Nothing could bring me down now

hat everything was clicking for me.

The only deterrent to my success was bad headaches that were coming to me on a consistent basis. I treated them as a mere bag of popcorn at the movies, the usual for a football player.

Coach Robinson and the rest of the coaching staff told us that we all did okay for our first game. He gave off the impression that it wasn't great, yet still could have been worse. They also said we needed to improve our conditioning, because we looked tired on the field.

"We will do more conditioning from now on in practice starting next week! Some of y'all look winded during the game. That's not only on you guys, that's also on us coaches too," reported one of the coaches.

Coach Robinson and the rest of the coaching staff had both squads do bleacher running; the ultimate stair master at Curt Flood Field. The bleachers at Curt Flood are wooden, and broken down as if termites were eating away at them by the hour. A player could fall into the temple of doom at any moment.

Coach Robinson told us specifically that we were to stay in the same order. The lines of the JV and varsity were mixed in together. The fortune in my cookie... Coach Robinson ordered me to fall in line right in front of Dewayne!

We were instructed to run up and down the bleachers for ten minutes. A little more than halfway through I started to winded and tired. I chugged along back

down the steps to get back in line. Dewayne, behind me, was done

going up. He beat me back down too. When it was my turn to go, he just

nodded, and proceeded to go.

Coach Robinson caught within seconds that we went out of

order and said, "I'm adding five minutes to this. I told y'all to stay in the

same order!"

"Who went out of order?" asked several players

simultaneously and sporadically out of breath.

"Dewayne went before Wes," Coach Robinson pointed

out like a snitch.

Everyone glanced at Dewayne and me.

Somehow I knew the glares were pierced deeper on me, again!

Before anyone gave me a hard time verbally, I was able to speak out, barely speaking in full sentences, "He knew I didn't go yet, so don't look at me! This ain't my fault!"

That practice seemed like it went on forever. After the bleacher run was over, we did wind sprints on the field, following more agility drills. Finally towards the end of practice, when everyone was exhausted, we broke off into JV and varsity. The coaches had us review plays we ran in the game at walking speed. They added some ideas and formations, and we corrected the plays we ran in the ame, all based on what the coaches saw on the film.

Once the strategy session was over, the finish line was waiting back at the school. We all took off running to the locker room, not looking back as if turning back would turn us all into salt.

**

When it came time for the weather to change I learned about yet another aspect of football I had to adapt to. Rainy days were long, even outside of playing football. When it came to gym class, it always meant being inside. My thoughts throughout the day centered-around hoping the coaches felt the same way about football practice.

The rain was coming down harder than a principal who had come down on a misguided student. When we all ran outside, hoping for the cancellation of practice, there was Coach Robinson outside the locker room preparing for practice.

"There's no practice today, right coach?" most of JV said in unison leaning out the hallway door.

"Why wouldn't there be practice?"

"It's raining!" we all exclaimed.

"What does that mean?" Coach Robinson responded sarcastically.

"This is football weather!" Coach Robinson and some of the varsity players would often proclaim when it rained.

Some people love playing or watching sports like football or soccer in the rain. Others like former ESPN columnist and debater on ESPN *First Take*, now currently on *Fox Sports One*, Skip Bayless, thinks that weather should never impact, or play a factor in the game.

"I can't stand seeing the great game of football being reduced to an unwatchable joke by snowstorms, or driving rain, or howling wind chill," Bayless expressed in one of his sports columns for ESPN.

Dad would often tell me stories about his football practices in the rain too. He thought they were always fun. He especially liked performing his coaches' special set of drills one being called "reindeers" where players had to run, slide, and then get back up. Dad claimed that the mud and rain always made the drill more enjoyable for them.

As for me, I always felt I couldn't mentally force myself to go full speed. I didn't want to slip and fall. I had never broken any bones, or torn anything. The thought of such an injury was enough for me to not want the experience. I heard so many stories about the pain it is something I never want to recover from. Running in the rain and trying to maintain a full speed mentality wasn't happening. That is the wrong way to play football regardless of the conditions.

Whenever I watched an event on television that was played in the rain, mostly baseball, because again I wasn't big on watching football, I found it entertaining. I wanted to observe how professional players responded to having to play with a different foil in a sport. I was fascinated to view on television

he adjustments the best athletes in the world would have to make. These
ros are on the biggest stages, with millions of viewers being forced to
nake adjustments in some of the most difficult weather and still play at
high level regardless.

***

Reflecting on my football career to that point, I felt I was on
pace to play at a high level all the time now. I was having a great start
to my week of practice, which lasted throughout. The coaches and my
teammates noticed my improvements on the field. What really made
me proud was the recognition the varsity players were giving me.

On Friday we had a regular practice, even though we didn't
have a game that week. We had our usual practice with varsity.
During our linemen drills, the varsity linemen even let me lead in our

rally-cry breakdowns before and after the drills were done.

"Let's go and finish out the rest of these drills! It's hot and we tired, but we gotta push through! Get better on three, get better on me!" I shouted.

I was definitely flying around the practice field that week like I had the best haircut on the block. I wasn't blowing up the varsity players tackling wise, still, I was withstanding their blows, holding my own, and made plenty of standout plays. Friday's practice ended, and as I was walking to the sideline to put my running shoes on, out of nowhere, the whole Mustang family dumped the rest of our practice water on me. It was as if I had won the Super Bowl!

"I'm not the coach!" I yelled, smiling.

The water was cold. With the chill of the light breeze blowing, along with the lingering sweat on my skin, I had the shivers for a couple minutes. It felt refreshing after a rigorous week. I turned around and could see the coaches laughing and smiling. They were in on it too! The feelings I had surging through my veins in that moment were indescribable. I wanted this feeling to remain in my psyche, and carry me throughout the rest of the season.

Coach Davis shouted from where the coaches were standing, "That's how you know for sure you've been accepted as a player on this team!"

***

Coach Robinson had both JV and varsity go head up all week. He wanted us to look polished and ready to play Moreau Catholic High School when it came game time. It was going to be a shortened week because this was a Friday night-lights game. Coach Robinson, and the other coaches rode JV players like we were his varsity team that week.

Now that I somewhat made a name for myself, the coaches looked at me as one of the guys o lead by example. It was no longer acceptable to slip to the back of the line to avoid going up against the best during drills.

Consequently I went up with Dewayne and he laid me out continuously. It was like I was a fly and Dewayne was a fly swatter trying to kill me for flying near his food.

It felt as if every hit Dewayne put on me took a little bit off my life. He laid one hit on me that left me stunned on the ground for a few seconds.

I was in so much pain I reached the point where I didn't want to get up. I broke out in tears, helmet on and all.

Coach B.J. had to pull me aside to try and keep my morale up. He offered a better way to go about tackling Dewayne. Not that there was a special antidote that was going to assist me in slaying Dewayne. In my head I thought, *"How am I always paired with this dude anyway?"* So many thoughts were going through my mind. I had to bite down on my mouthpiece to gather myself. That, or strip out of my gear, walk off and quit.

Quitting was the only true way to rid myself of all my physical and emotional pain. That was a telling thought after the rough and rugged practices. Sometimes I would cry to my parents about how I was feeling. I wanted to quit so badly in those: prisoner of the moment realizations. In the back of my mind though, I knew I would never quit voluntarily.

Coach Robinson didn't care that we were all getting punch drunk like a boxer. It was time for JV to get better. Coach Robinson yelled at me while I was slowing getting up from the truck that hit me on the field, "Come on Wes, you're going to have to get lower, and hit harder than that! Everyone go take a water break!"

He walked over to me and said, "I see you got a little choked up back there," phrasing it as if it didn't warrant my response. With my eyes still moist, I finally let out, "I'm trying to hit harder Coach," I said, as we both walked to the sideline.

"That's what I want to hear!"

"No problem Coach," I said, with an exhausted expression on my face.

"I like how you go about your business, and allow us to coach you up Wes."

"I was always raised like that Coach. My parents have always taught me; any job you do don't make excuses, just get it done."

"See, if more people had an attitude like yours, Wes, the world would be more productive."

He never brought up the fact that I was actually crying during the last drill. This meant one of two things; one, he didn't care, or two, it was just tough love and he knew it happens in sports. By this point my stress wasn't only caused by playing football, it was the totality of everything.

My grades were slipping, and everyday life was starting to take a toll on me.

"Thanks Coach," I said, after wiping excess water from my lips. Then I put my helmet back on to prepare for the next set of drills.

***

When it was finally time to face the Moreau Mariners, I felt nothing could stop me. I was assured of my starting spot this time. I was going to take care of business in the same way I had proven I could during the end of the last game. The Mariners team wasn't known to be good on paper, so even though we were discouraged from doing so, I was already marking them down as a win.

I was acquainted with a couple of people who enrolled at Moreau as freshmen. I could hear whispers from students on the Mariners campus as my teammates

and I marched from our bus to the field asking, "Is that Wesley?"

I needed to maintain my focus without getting distracted,

so when a few people called out my name, I kept looking straight

ahead without acknowledging them.

"You know people here Wesley?" Coach

B.J. asked.

"Yeah I do Coach," implying I wanted to leave it at that.

We did our warm-up routine with everyone trying to get as

loose as possible. The last warm-up activity we did after every stretch was

MUSTANG jumping jacks. I could tell from how loud and proud

we warmed up, I wasn't the only player hyped for this game. I'm sure the whole Moreau campus could hear us!

MUSTANG jumping jacks would always start with a rotating player shouting, "Six clap, six clap, ready? Hit!"

Then we would all hit our thigh pads like drums, six times. As soon as they started there would be a two-clap count in between each letter too.

"WE GOT MUSTANG JUMPING JACKS! READY? BEGIN! M, U, S, T, A, N, G, S! WHAT'S THAT SPELL? MUSTANGS! BRING IT IN!"

Something about knowing I was starting in the game made my adrenaline pump more than usual. I was trying to be as crisp as a cookie while I warmed-up, and stretched. Keying in on all my form tackling techniques. I couldn't allow any small mistakes ruining the bigger goal. I wanted perfection and to give my teammates my all this game. To my surprise we were trailing seven to zero at halftime. I was doing okay. I wasn't making the impact I strived for though. There was always more I could have been doing.

The second half started with the Moreau Mariners returning the kickoff to our end zone for a touchdown. I was furious our special teams allowed it to happen. At least I was in the smoothie blender to take accountancy for the score though.

***

Midway through the fourth quarter I had to make a move up to the second level of the field fter knocking my man down. I was weaving through the opening I

reated and tripped in a hole that had been in the dirt of the field.

Anyone who has ever played on Moreau's field in years past knows

about the holes in the grass and dirt everywhere. My ankle was

hurting. Then a blob of players landed on my ankle after the play was

over.

"I need a sub, I rolled my ankle," I shouted to the sidelines

frantically.

Coach Montenes got me a sub and I limped out of the game.

He gave me an option to go back in five minutes later.

Regretfully as I looked up at a devastating scoreboard,

seventeen to seven at that point, I replied, "Coach my ankle still

hurts, and I don't

think I'll be able to get back in this one," showcasing the bag of ice in my hand.

If I had known what I know now from listening to former NFL players on ESPN *First Take* like Lomas Brown, Hugh Douglas, and others, that if a player is hurt, not injured, they should never give up their spot to come out of a game. Just get some treatment and get back out on the field as fast as possible. I should have responded by throwing the ice down and running back on the field. I didn't. I sat out to watch the rest of the game.

That game ended terribly, still Coach Montenes told us, "Go home and reflect on our loss, and be ready to go on Monday."

I wasn't LeBron James after getting beat by the Orlando Magic in the Eastern Conference

Finals, but I was beginning to think how many times I'd

actually hear those words this season.

***

When I woke up Sunday morning, I found myself with yet

another headache. I told Mom and she gave me some Advil.

"Maybe you should go back to bed and see if you feel

better later," she suggested.

I went back to sleep and slept until about one in the afternoon.

I should have never listened to Mom because whenever I go back to sleep,

I always sleep longer than I want to. The day was pretty much over as far

as making plans. I relaxed at home until it was time for bed.

***

It was about two in the morning when I woke up from

my sleep. I felt dizzy and nauseous. I

thought maybe a drink would help, so I crept downstairs like a car cylinder, trying not to wake up anyone. I got a drink and also snuck a piece of Mom's' delicious cake. I slowly walked through our living room to go back upstairs. I was still feeling a little light headed when it happened. I didn't pass out; I just collapsed to the floor. I haltingly got up and worked my way over to our couch to sit up.

I tried to calm my headache down, to no avail. I started sobbing. I could barely take the pain I was feeling. Finally, like a grandfather's' clock bell piece, I managed to wobble back up the stairs to tell my parents what was going on. They both got up out of bed to help me walk in my room to lie back down.

The headache was throbbing now. My parents tried every method they knew to treat it. Dad decided to stay by my bedside for the remainder of the night. In my head I thought, '*I feel like I am five years old again, with my dad here next to me.*'

It took about two hours for my headache to ease off enough for me to fall back asleep. That night was as dramatic for me as if I was sitting through a Shakespeare play. My parents chose not to wake me up for school the next morning. When I finally woke up, it was already eight thirty, (school started at eight.) I jetted downstairs to find Dad walking out the door for work, and Mom on the phone talking to someone.

When she finally got off the phone I asked her, "Why didn't you wake me up for school?"

"I need to take you to the doctor, so you're going to be late to school. That was too bad of a headache last night to let it go."

"I guess you're right Mom. When is my appointment?"

"It is at ten thirty. Go get dressed so we can get there on time."

I went back upstairs, got dressed, and took care of some other things to pass the time. Soon after I went back downstairs to find Mom ready to leave.

As we were zooming up the highway Mom asked, "So how do you feel now?"

"I guess I'm alright, I don't have a headache anymore."

***

When we arrived at Kaiser Permanente in Hayward, I was seen immediately so they could run numerous tests on my head. The multiple tests lasted about forty-five minutes. They also did balance and coordination tests that I had never seen or heard of before. While the medical staff were wrapping up their findings the lead doctor called Mom and I into a private room to talk about what the problem was.

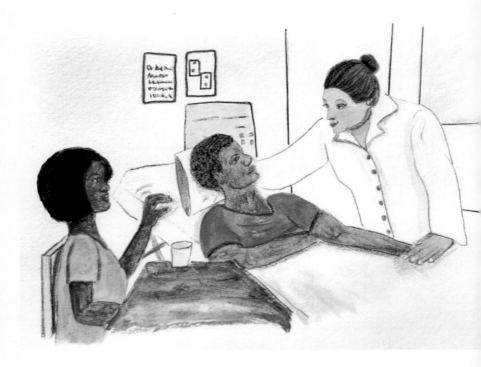

The Doctor started off by saying, "I hate to be the one to deliver this bad news, but someone has to. After we reviewed the tests we ran on your head we discovered you have hydrocephalus."

"Hydro what?" Mom and I responded in unison.

"Hydrocephalus," the doctor repeated. "We are going to have to send Wesley up to the Kaiser in Oakland to do even more tests on him."

Mom broke out in tears. I was still in shock from what the doctor said.

"What does that mean?" I asked in confusion.

"Well hydrocephalus is where the brain has too much pressure forced upon it. The fluid around your brain builds up, and gets clogged, causing your headaches to explain it simply. Again, I hate to say it, but I think you've played your last down on the football field," the doctor concluded.

Mom, still in tears, called Dad at work. She told him to get to the hospital immediately. Dad raced to the hospital to see what the problem was.

She was like all good moms are when it comes to something worrisome regarding their child; they can get uncontrollably emotional. Listening to the doctors was quickly making her uneasy. When Dad arrived he recognized Mom's distress and asked if there was a separate room he and the doctor could speak in alone. There he acquired the necessary understanding of hydrocephalus. After about fifteen minutes Dad and the doctor returned to where Mom and I were waiting.

For Dad a light bulb went off about many of the interesting issues I faced as a child. These issues included my lifetime bouts with migraine headaches and my occasional difficulties playing in the outfield during baseball seasons; being unable to properly locate fly balls. These concerns, along with other little things, suddenly made sense!

Like the doctor said, I had to go up to Oakland to get more test done. The doctor assured me that these were some of the best neurology doctors in the country and I had nothing to worry about. I got to ride in an ambulance for the first time, which was pretty cool. My parents couldn't ride with me, but a couple of medics were sitting next to me, keeping me relaxed.

We arrived at Kaiser of Oakland where they immediately put me in a room. What we thought would be a short visit to the doctor's' office turned into a weeklong hotel stay at the hospital. It was scary! The doctors ran all types of test on me, including what's called a magnetic resonance imaging, or MRI for short.

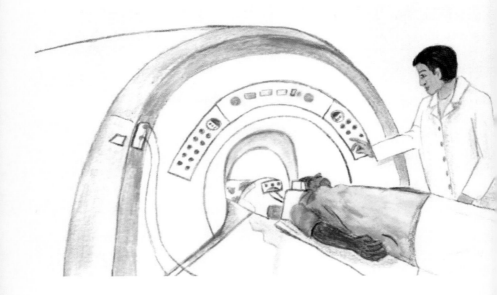

I also had to get a CT scan. Both machines are huge and make a ton of noise, like being in a construction zone. It almost feels like it is going to eat you alive! Even so, all an MRI does is analyze the water molecules in a person's body. It can take anywhere between thirty to forty-five minutes to complete. A CT scan gives more bony details, and examines a person's organs.

I was blessed to have Mom stay with me the entire time, with Dad either a short distance, or phone call away. Other family, and friends periodically throughout the week checked on me too. The doctors tested my balance and coordination. I was asked to squeeze my doctor's two fingers together for testing my hand strength. Then I had to allow the doctors to shine a bright light in my eyes to assess how my eyes reacted. I was also hooked up to an I.V. while I lied in my hospital bed.

Doctors and nurses came and went from my room to examine any changes. They took my blood pressure throughout the day, and night. Waking me up when they came in, even if I was sleeping.

Everything was happening around me, but all I

could think about were the words my doctor told me, '*No more*

football.'

***

When I got back to school, everyone was wondering what was

wrong. It was all a blur to me though. I couldn't believe all that had

transpired in the past week of my life. I explained to them what the

doctors said and how I was told I couldn't play football anymore. My

friends and teammates were all at a loss of words. We all knew they

would have to work even harder now that I wasn't going to be playing.

My season, and my football career were over! There was nothing I could

do!

***

I committed to football my freshman year of high school, and I was going to stick with it until I was a senior. Even though I learned I had a condition that would keep me from playing on the field, I wasn't going to let that keep me from *being* on the field. Coach Robinson allowed me to help the football program every weekend the Mustangs had a game.

Soon after, the athletic director took notice of me. He asked if I wouldn't mind helping him during home games by being a part of the chain gang. The athletic director's name was Mr. Smith. Mr. Smith was an older European American gentlemen who had been a part of St. Elizabeth dating back to the early seventies. He had been my fifth grade elementary school teacher's, teacher dating back to the late 80's, and early 90's!

In a way to bring this side story full circle, he actually had close ties with my teacher, as did I. At the time though, I was unaware of this association. The connection became apparent over the years through the many stories that both Mr. Smith, and my former teacher shared with me. What I did know at that time was that Mr. Smith taught tenth grade physical education. I was also aware he sold doughnuts to students during break. Mr. Smith was an overall friendly soul. Initially, when he asked me to help with the chains, I had no problem accepting his invitation.

Being a part of the chain gang gave me an all access pass to the action as opposed to a seat in the stands. I was able to move up and down the field during the games marking the downs for both teams. This was a different kind of football participation. I would not have been exposed to this kind of inside experience had I not been diagnosed with hydrocephalus.

Mr. Smith gave me seven hours of community service for helping him with each home game. That in itself was worth my efforts because I needed one hundred community service hours to graduate.

It was never about the community service hours though. Nor was it about the unprecedented access to the field. It was about the overall experience. It was about going to games, being on the field and watching my teammates play football.

It was nice to know, in a different way, that I was a part of a football program that went to three consecutive championship games. Our team won two of the three games. The Varsity team had a win during my sophomore year, a loss my junior year, and another win during my senior year! All three of our championship games were played against the St. Patrick-St. Vincent Bruins. We all received championship rings and all the glory that came with them.

The championship ring I was awarded, in my senior season is special, and near to my heart. I declined to buy the ring my sophomore year, but I put a lot of value in the senior ring because it represented an accumulation of the four years I put into the sport.

Beginning with my freshman year as a rookie player

on JV, through the trials and accomplishments I achieved on my way to becoming a senior. I felt like a real champion for winning the title *with* my teammates who actually played on the field.

The rings were customized for each individual. I made sure to have my freshmen number, seventy, engraved on one side. On the other side it reads, "small in number, big in heart."

Over the years, while we watched former and new teammates warm-up prior to games, Coach Robinson would periodically ask if I ever missed playing football.

Each time I would look up at him and smile, "I wouldn't be out here if I didn't coach."

Whenever I told him that, I would have flashbacks of everything I endured. I remembered the good and the bad. I'd recall the highs of my short career, the lows, and everything in between.

Even knowing my ultimate fate, I still wouldn't change my decision to play football. I will remember my experience for the rest of my life. Even though I never developed a great talent for the game. Had my fortunes been different and had I been allowed to stick with it, I know I could have possibly been one of the best football players Coach Robinson had ever coached. Even though God had other plans for me, I am, and will always be, a Mustang football player!

Quick Facts About Hydrocephalus

Source: hydroassoc.org

❖ Hydrocephalus affects approximately 1 million Americans, in every stage of life, from infants to the elderly. It affects people in all walks of life, from a socioeconomic background.

❖ One out of every 1,000 babies are born with hydrocephalus, making it as common as down syndrome and more common than spina bifida or brain tumors.

❖ Hydrocephalus is the most common reason for brain surgery in children.

❖ There is no medical therapy to treat hydrocephalus. The only effective treatments are surgical.

❖ While many people are helped by surgery, many more need further operations to stay well. Of the nearly 40,000 hydrocephalus operations performed annually (one every fifteen minutes), only 30% are the patient's first surgery to treat hydrocephalus.

❖ The medical cost for hydrocephalus are over $2 billion per year, yet the National Institutes of Health (NIH) invests less than $8 million per year in hydrocephalus research.

❖ A recent study estimates that 700,000 older Americans are living with normal pressure hydrocephalus (NPH). This disorder often goes undiagnosed and untreated, with an estimate that up to 80% of cases remain unrecognized.

- *Of the estimated 5.2 million individuals diagnosed with dementia, 5% are believed to have NPH, which is treatable.*
- *Accurately diagnosing adult hydrocephalus would save Medicare in excess of $184MM over five years.*
- *Hydrocephalus also goes undiagnosed and untreated in younger adults, leading to substantial workforce loss, and health care costs.*
- *Doctors are sometimes understandably reticent to take o complicated hydrocephalus cases, particular in adults, because little is known about the disorder. We don't always know what causes it, and we don't know yet how to make these people well.*
- *There are fewer than ten centers in the United States specializing in treating adults with hydrocephalus.*
- *Over the last 50 years, there has been no significant improvement in hydrocephalus treatment and no progress toward prevention and cure.*
- *Research is essential. At the very least, we need better treatments, with more positive long-term outcomes, and diagnostic tests that are accurate, cost-effective, and noninvasive.*

Glossary

BART: bay area rapid transit (train), San Francisco, CA Transit.

Bench press: A bodybuilding and weightlifting exercise in which a lifter lies on a bench with feet on the floor and raises a weight with both arms.

Center: Innermost linemen on the offensive line, responsible for snapping the ball to the quarterback, and blocking.

Chain gang: Crew that manages the signal poles on one of the sidelines. The chain gang, under the direction of the referee's, signals the referee's decisions. The crew does not make decisions.

Crows Feet: Small dots and lines used to indicate where a person grips a weightlifting bar.

CT Scan: Computed Tomography Scan is a type of x-ray that allows doctors to see the inside of a person's body at different angles to produce cross-sectional images or slices, of the bones, blood vessels, and soft tissues inside your body.

Defense: Pass defense. When the defense believes the opposing offense will pass the ball, they go into pass defense. Zone, where certain players (usually defensive backs and linebackers, though occasionally linemen as well) are assigned an area on the field that they are to cover.

Four point stance: Stance used by defensive linemen in American football to start a play. Stance requires two hands to touch the ground and knees bent in an athletic squat.

Gridiron: Another term for a football field.

Helmet: Consists of a hard plastic shell with thick padding inside, a facemask made of one or more plastic coated metal bars, and a chinstrap.

Hip and Thigh Pads: Are made of plastic and protect the hips, pelvis, and the tailbone. The pads are inserted into the pockets of a girdle worn under the football pants.

Jockstrap: An undergarment for supporting the male genitalia during any contact sport or rigorous physical activity.

Holding: The illegal straining of another player who is not in possession of the ball.

Holes (in the offensive line): Openings in the offensive line scheme for the running backs to move through.

Hydrocephalus: A condition in which fluid accumulates in the brain, typically in young children, enlarging the head and sometimes causing brain damage.

Incline press: The pectoralis major are comprised of a clavicle and a stern costal head, better known of as the upper and lower peck. The purpose of the incline press is to focus more of the work on the upper pecs.

JV: Junior Varsity, lower division for teams in high school.

Left and Right guard: Player who lines up between the center, and the tackles on the offensive, responsible for blocking.

Left and Right tackle: Position on the far left or right on the line responsible for blocking.

Linemen: A player who specializes in a play at the line of scrimmage. The linemen of a team currently in possession of the ball are offensive linemen. They block, and protect the quarterback from being hit by the defense.

Max out: **Maxing out is lifting the most possible weight a person can do in an exercise both in pounds, and or reps. If one reached their max they would be in an all out struggle and would not possibly be able to lift any more.**

Mouthpiece: A sometimes-rubbery guard for a player's mouth covering a row of a player's teeth.

MRI: Magnetic Resonance Imaging is a test that uses powerful magnets, radio waves, and a computer to make detailed pictures inside a person's body.

Offense: The offensive team is attempting to advance the ball down the field and score. The team consists of a quarterback, five offensive linemen, and a combination of running backs, wide receivers, and tight ends, depending on the formation being used by the offense on any given play.

Quarterback: Player positioned behind the center that directs an offensive play, and throws the ball.

Running back: Offensive position responsible for running the ball, and occasionally catch short passes out of the backfield.

Sack: Occurs when the quarterback is tackled behind the line of scrimmage before he can throw a forward pass.

Snapping: Is the backwards passing of the ball in American football at the start of a play from the line of scrimmage.

Special teams: Special teams in American football, units that are on the field during kicking plays.

Three point stance: Stance used by linemen and running backs in American football to start a play. Stance requires one hand to touch the ground with the other arm cocked back to the thigh/hip region.

Touchdown: A six point score made by carrying or passing the ball into the end zone of the opposing side, or by recovering there following a fumble, or blocked kick

Trenches: Referring to the space directly and around the offensive and defensive line.

Up-Downs: Running in place, then dropping to the ground to do a push-up and getting back up to repeat the action.

Varsity: Highest-level for high school sports.

Ventricles: Each of the four connected fluid filled cavities in the center of the brain.

Wide Receivers: The principal players in American football who catch passes.

Printed in Great Britain
by Amazon